A
Tallis Anthology

17 Anthems and Motets

Compiled by

JOHN MILSOM

Music Department
OXFORD UNIVERSITY PRESS
Oxford and New York

Oxford University Press, Walton Street, Oxford OX2 6DP, England
Oxford University Press, 200 Madison Avenue, New York, NY 10016, USA

Oxford is a trade mark of Oxford University Press

© *Oxford University Press 1992*

ISBN 0 19 353410 X

CONTENTS

1	Audivi vocem de caelo	*page*	1
2	Derelinquit impius		9
3	Hear the voice and prayer		19
4	If ye love me		25
5	In ieiunio et fletu		28
6	In manus tuas		36
7	Laudate Dominum		40
8	Mihi autem nimis		54
9	O Lord, give thy Holy Spirit		60
10	O Lord, in thee is all my trust		64
11	O nata lux		74
12	O sacrum convivium		77
13	O salutaris hostia		87
14	Purge me, O Lord		95
15	Salvator mundi		99
16	Te lucis ante terminum		107
17	Verily, verily, I say unto you		113

INTRODUCTION

Born in the first decade of the sixteenth century, Thomas Tallis was trained as a singing-man and keyboard player, and attained his first professional position as organist at Dover Priory when barely out of his teens. Short periods of employment followed in London, at Waltham Abbey in Essex, and at Canterbury Cathedral; but all those posts merely prefaced the main body of his career. By 1545 Tallis had entered the service of the Chapel Royal, England's foremost choral foundation. It was with this institution that he remained until his death forty years later, actively composing music until the 1570s. In the words of his epitaph:

> He serv'd long Tyme in Chappell with grete prayse,
> Fower Sovereygnes Reygnes (a Thing not often seen)
> I mean Kyng Henry and Prynce Edward's Dayes,
> Quene Mary, and Elizabeth our Quene.

Under Henry VIII, plainchant and polyphony for the Catholic rite dominated Tallis's daily life. In the reign of Henry's youngest child, Edward VI, the Chapel Royal adopted Protestant forms of worship as stipulated by the earliest versions of *The Book of Common Prayer*. Queen Mary, Henry's daughter by his first wife, Katherine of Aragon, resolutely restored England to the Catholic faith of her mother, whose divorce from Henry had occasioned England's break with the Church of Rome. Elizabeth's personal religious persuasion remains the subject of debate, but under her monarchy England officially returned to *The Book of Common Prayer*.

Had Tallis written music only for performance in churches, his surviving works might have fallen neatly into four chronological layers corresponding to those 'Fower Sovereygnes Reygnes'. But Tallis, like his younger colleague William Byrd, evidently never relinquished the Catholic faith, and composed ostensibly Catholic works even after Elizabeth's accession. The destination of his late motets is uncertain: some may have been used by the Chapel Royal, where Latin was tolerated; others were more likely composed for Catholic circles, to be sung for devotional recreation. Some survive only in manuscripts copied by individuals for their private use. Others were published by Tallis and Byrd in 1575 in a book titled *Cantiones, quae ab argumento sacrae vocantur*—'Songs which by subject-matter are called sacred'. The dedication is to Elizabeth, but there is no mention of performance by the Chapel Royal or church choirs.

The present anthology makes no attempt to show the full breadth of Tallis's achievement. If anything, it avoids works that are strictly liturgical, such as Masses and settings of ritual texts from the Roman Kalendar. The only exception is *Audivi vocem de caelo*, written either late in Henry VIII's reign or during Mary's, which is a Matins Responsory for the feast of All Saints. The remaining works fall into three categories, all of them remote from or peripheral to the liturgy: anthems, devotional partsongs, and motets.

The Book of Common Prayer, at least in the forms in which Tallis knew it, was vague about the role of the anthem, and left the selection of texts to the clergy. At least two of the anthems included here, *Hear the voice and prayer* and *If ye love me*, were being sung in churches during Edward VI's reign, presumably occupying the same position they still do in Anglican worship today: preceding the concluding prayers at Evensong. Two further anthems, *O Lord, give thy Holy Spirit* and *Verily, verily, I say unto you*, are likely to be later works, to judge from their source-distribution and style.

Tallis's devotional partsongs differ from his true anthems more on account of their texts (which are verse rather than prose) than their musical content. Almost certainly a blurring of function already existed in the composer's lifetime: several of Tallis's anthems are found in Elizabethan music-books destined for the chamber rather than the church, while one of the partsongs—*O Lord, in Thee is all my trust*—appears in books that may have been used during church services. The somewhat moral tone of *Purge me, O Lord* more obviously suggests the home rather than the chapel.

Pride of place in this anthology is given to Tallis's Elizabethan motets, his crowning achievement. Several of these have close connections with the Roman liturgy, but none may fairly be said to have been composed for it—not even the two tiny settings of the Compline hymn *Te lucis ante terminum*, which, like *Audivi vocem de caelo*, quote plainchant melodies and need chant to be completed. Also close to the liturgy, though lacking a plainchant basis, are *O sacrum convivium* and *O salutaris hostia*, which might have been sung as Eucharistic hymns by the Chapel Royal. Devotional motets such as *In manus tuas, Mihi autem nimis, Salvator mundi*, and *O nata lux* make acceptable Latin-texted anthems for performance at Evensong. The more ebullient *Laudate Dominum* could have been sung as a celebratory piece on a state occasion. Whatever their original function, however, we can be sure that all these motets were also performed in domestic surroundings, either by single voices, household instruments (most commonly viols), or a mixture of the two.

Two motets can hardly have been welcome even within the tolerant privacy of Elizabeth's Chapel Royal. It is tempting to read *Derelinquit impius* through the eyes of Catholics of the period, with its plea for the wicked to forsake their paths and return to the Lord. More transparent still is the extraordinary *In ieiunio et fletu*, whose weeping priests plead for their heritage not to be destroyed. These passionate works, which seem to transcend the normal conditions of Tallis's employment and hint at personal convictions, may be the last he wrote.

John Milsom (Oxford, 1991)

Audivi vocem de caelo

Edited by John Milsom
Matins Responsory, All Saints

THOMAS TALLIS
(*c.*1505–85)

Translation: I heard a voice coming from heaven: Come, all you most wise virgins; store up the oil in your vessels until the bridegroom comes. At midnight the cry broke forth: Behold, the bridegroom comes! Store up the oil in your vessels until the bridegroom comes.

46

[nit, ve] — — — — — — — nit.

— — — — — — — — nit.

ve] — — — — — — nit.

— — — — — nit.

B

O - le - um re - con - di - te in va — — — sis___ ves - tris

dum spon — — — sus___ ad - ve - ne — — rit.___

Sources

Polyphony: London, British Library, Additional MSS 17802–5, ff. 101v, 106, 104v, 98 (mid-16th century).

Plainchant: *Antiphonarii ad usum Sarum volumen secundum: vulgo pars aestivalis nuncupata* (Paris, 1520), corrected and emended in accordance with various late medieval manuscript copies of the Sarum Antiphonal.

Commentary

In the Sarum rite the plainchant melody of 'Audivi vocem de caelo' was sung in alternation by boys and full choir: five boys stationed at the steps of the choir sang the portions of text that Tallis set to polyphony, while the passages he left as chant were sung tutti. Whether or not Tallis's polyphony was intended for unbroken voices is unclear. The present edition can comfortably be transposed up a third from the printed pitch.

Derelinquit impius

Edited by John Milsom

Matins Responsory, first Sunday in Lent (Roman rite)

THOMAS TALLIS
(*c*.1505–85)

Source: William Byrd and Thomas Tallis, *Cantiones . . . sacrae* (London, 1575), no. 13.
Translation: The wicked man forsakes his ways, and the unrighteous man his thoughts; and let him return unto the Lord, and He will have mercy upon him: for the Lord our God is gracious and merciful, and ever ready to relent when he threatens disaster.

Hear the voice and prayer

Edited by John Milsom
1 Kings 8: 28–30

THOMAS TALLIS
(c.1505–85)

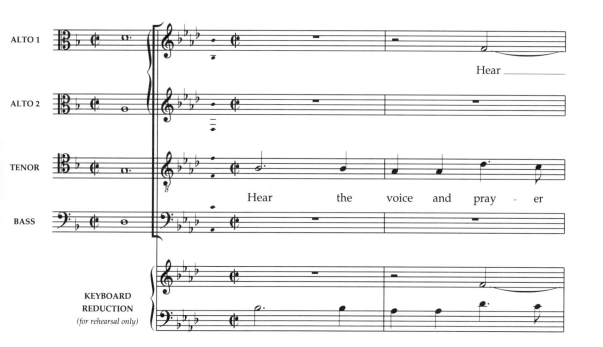

Sources

A Oxford, Bodleian Library, MSS Mus. Sch. e. 420–2 (three partbooks from a set of four, lacking Tenor; copied *c.*1550).

B London, British Library, Additional MS 15166 (Treble partbook, *c.*1570).

C John Day, *Certaine Notes* (London, 1560/1565) and *Mornyng and Evenyng Prayer* (London, 1565).

D The Chirk Castle partbooks: New York, Public Library, MS Mus. Res. *MNZ [Chirk] (copied *c.*1620–35).

Other, later sources are listed in Ralph T. Daniel and Peter Le Huray, *The Sources of English Church Music 1549–1660*, Early English Church Music, Supplementary Volume 1 (London, 1972); these have not been consulted.

Commentary

No source transmits a better reading of this anthem than **A**, which is the earliest extant but which lacks its Tenor partbook. In this edition, **A** is followed for the Alto 1, Alto 2, and Bass parts; the Tenor has been reconstructed using sources **C** and **D**, not all of whose readings have been accepted. Accidentals in small type are either absent from **A** but present in other sources, or are missing in all sources and supplied editorially. Further viable accidentals stated or implied by **C** and **D** are shown in footnotes, and are optional. Other variant readings in sources **B**, **C**, and **D**, and obvious copying errors in **A**, have not been reported.

¹ **C**: D natural implied   ² **C, D**: D natural   ³ **D**: D flat implied

[4] **C**: D natural implied   [5] **D**: E natural; next note E flat

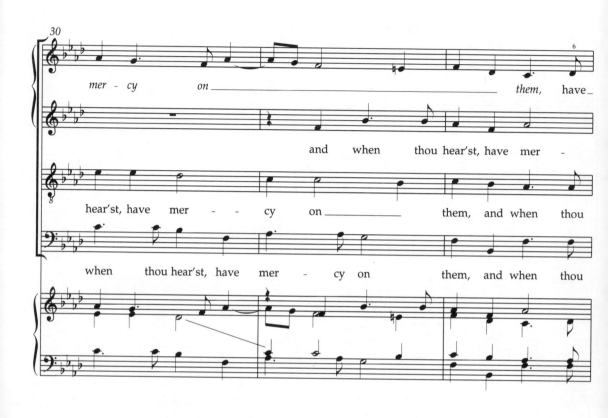

mer - cy on _____ them, have _

and when thou hear'st, have mer -

hear'st, have mer - - cy on _____ them, and when thou

when thou hear'st, have mer - cy on them, and when thou

_ mer - cy _ on _ them; _ them.

- cy on _____ them; that thine eyes may them.

hear'st, have mer - cy _ on _____ them; that thine _ them.

hear'st, have mer - cy on _____ them; _ them.

[6] C: D naturals implied

[7] All sources express this chord as a semibreve (or longer value) with fermata. Possibly Alto 1, Tenor, and Bass should hold notes over into bar 35.

If ye love me

Edited by Peter Le Huray
John 14: 15–17

THOMAS TALLIS
(*c*.1505–85)

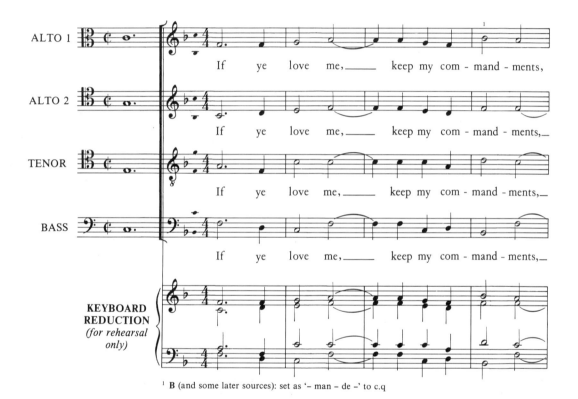

ALTO 1 — If ye love me,_____ keep my com - mand - ments,

ALTO 2 — If ye love me,_____ keep my com - mand - ments,_____

TENOR — If ye love me,_____ keep my com - mand - ments,_____

BASS — If ye love me,_____ keep my com - mand - ments,_____

**KEYBOARD
REDUCTION**
(*for rehearsal
only*)

[1] **B** (and some later sources): set as '– man – de –' to c.q

Sources

A *Certaine notes set forth in foure and three parts* (London, 1560)/*Mornyng and evenyng prayer and Communion, set forthe in foure partes* (London, 1565).

B Oxford, Bodleian Library, MSS Mus. Sch. e. 420–2: the 'Wanley' partbooks, *c*.1546–9; three partbooks from a set of four, lacking the Tenor book.

This anthem is also found in Jacobean and later sources. For details of those manuscripts and their readings, see *Thomas Tallis: English Sacred Music: 1 Anthems*, ed. Leonard Ellinwood, rev. Paul Doe, *Early English Church Music*, 12 (London, 1973), no. 3.

This edition has been reprinted with minor modifications from *The Treasury of English Church Music*, vol. 2, by permission of Blandford Press Ltd.

² **B:** cA for qq AB♭   ³ **B:** c c-rest for m

In ieiunio et fletu

Edited by Peter le Huray and David Willcocks

Matins Responsory, first Sunday in Lent

THOMAS TALLIS
(*c.*1505–85)

Source: William Byrd and Thomas Tallis, *Cantiones . . . sacrae.* (London, 1575), no. 26.

Translation: Fasting and weeping, the priests shall pray: Spare thy people, Lord, and give not thy heritage over to destruction. Between the porch and the altar, the priests shall pray: Spare thy people.

In manus tuas

Edited by
John Milsom

THOMAS TALLIS
(*c*.1505–85)

Compline Responsory

Source: William Byrd and Thomas Tallis, *Cantiones . . . sacrae* (London, 1575), no.3.
Translation: Into thy hands, O Lord, I commend my spirit; thou hast redeemed me, Lord, God of truth.

¹ Source: 'me-' aligned under G; the edition follows the placement of bar 19

² Text placement: the discrepancy with bar 24 may be intentional

Laudate Dominum

Edited by Alan Brown
Psalm 116 (117), with *Gloria Patri*

THOMAS TALLIS
(*c*.1505–85)

Translation

Praise the Lord, all nations; praise him, all peoples. For his loving-kindness towards us is strong, and the truth of the Lord endures for ever. Glory to the Father, and to the Son, and to the Holy Spirit: as it was in the beginning, is now and shall be always, for ever and ever. Amen.

Sources

A Oxford, Christ Church, Mus. 979–83, no.40 (five partbooks from a set of six, lacking Tenor; hand of John Baldwin, late 16th century).

B Oxford, Bodleian Library, Tenbury MS 1486, f.3, and privately owned 'Willmott' MS, unfoliated (Tenor, bars 18–end, and Alto 1 respectively; hand of John Sadler, dated 1591).

Sources **C** to **F** are from the Paston collection and may be dated *c*.1600–1610.

C Oxford, Bodleian Library, Tenbury MSS 341–4, f.14v etc. (four partbooks from a set of five, lacking Bass).

D Oxford, Bodleian library, Tenbury MSS 369–73, f.35v (complete set of five partbooks).

E Chelmsford, Essex County Record Office, MS D/DP.Z6/1, f.36 (Bass only).

F London, Royal College of Music, MS 2089, f.15 (lute arr. of voices II–V, a minor third above original pitch).

Critical Commentary

Source **A** lacks accidentals for A1, 19.2; A2, 21.3; A2, 37.4; A1, 51.3. Accidentals to the following are supported by **F** but are absent from the other sources: T, 14.4; A1, 15.3; T, 20.4; A1, 38.4; A2, 51.2; A1, 53.4. The following are naturals in **F**: T, 27.3; A2, 33.4.

A1, 13.4, **B,C,D**: G for A / B, 28.2–4, **D, E**: su⌐–per^{nx}/ A2, 46.3–47.3, **A**: –ni^{cc}ma^m–net· in ^{c}/ T, 100.2–101.2, **C,D**: –rum^q A–$^{qqm.m}$

[1] 88.2–89.3, **C**, **D**: saec– cuq– lo –mcm

[2] 91.2–92.4, **B**: sae – cu – locq– rum, sae – cu – lo – ; **C**, **D**: et in sae – cu – la sae – cu – lo –

Mihi autem nimis

Edited by Jason Smart
Psalm 139:17

THOMAS TALLIS
(*c.*1505–85)

Translation

How dear are thy counsels unto me, O God: O how great is the sum of them!

Sources

A William Byrd and Thomas Tallis, *Cantiones . . . sacrae* (London, 1575), no. 7.

B London, British Library, Add. MS. 29247 (early 17th cent.), f.9. An arrangement of the lowest four voices for lute. Not collated for this edition.

Critical Commentary

T, 23.2: New line; original key signature has B flat only, implying G natural in the edition from here onwards/ S, 26.6: underlay '–o–' to qC (but c.f. bar 32)/ B, 28.1: New line; original key signature B flat and E flat, implying G flat in the edition from here onwards

O Lord, give thy Holy Spirit

Edited by John Milsom
Text: from Lidley's Prayers

THOMAS TALLIS
(c.1505–85)

¹D: ♯ ² D: ♯ ³ D: ♯ ⁴ D: ♮

Sources

A London, British Library, Additional MS 15166 (*c.*1570): S only.

B New York, Public Library, Drexel MSS 4180–3 (*c.*1620): all four voices.

C London, British Library, Additional MS 29289 (*c.*1625): A only.

D John Barnard, *The first Book of Selected Church Musick* (London, 1641): all four voices.

E Oxford, Bodleian Library, Tenbury MS 1382 (*c.*1617): T only.

Critical Commentary

The edition is based on sources **A** and **B**. Source **D** is more generous in its provision of accidentals, but since it may reflect seventeenth-century taste rather than Tallis's intentions, accidentals unique to **D** have been suppressed and are recorded as footnotes. The sources also disagree over the need to repeat the closing section of the anthem (bars 11–29). Substantive variants are recorded below.

S, 2.3–3.1, **A**: cm; 2.3–3.2, **B**: cA cA mG sharp; both sources require the word 'Spirit' to be sung as two syllables/B, 7.2, **B**:C/A, 28.3–29.1, **C, D**:m/B, 28.3–29.1, **B**:m.c

O Lord, in thee is all my trust

Edited by John Milsom
Words: anon., *c*.1550

THOMAS TALLIS
(*c*.1505–85)

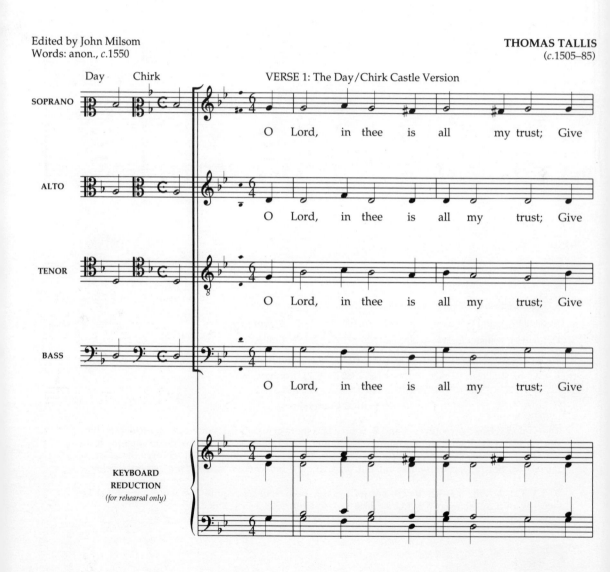

[3] shent: free   [4] sith: since

VERSE 2: The 'Parsons's Psalter' Version

No, no, not so, thy will is bent To deal with sin - ners
No, no, not so, thy will is bent To deal with sin - ners
No, no, not so, thy will is bent To deal with sin - ners
No, no, not so, thy will is bent To deal with sin - ners

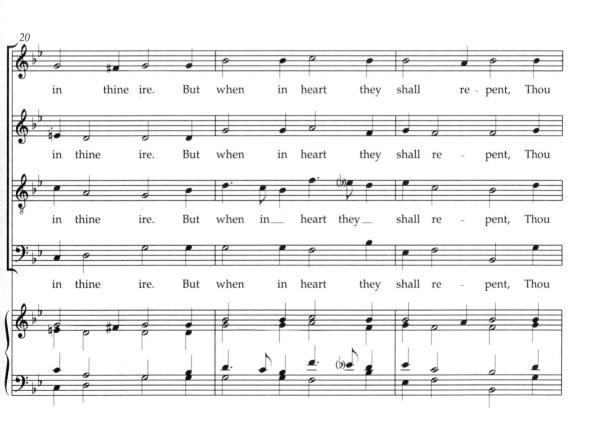

in thine ire. But when in heart they shall re - pent, Thou
in thine ire. But when in heart they shall re - pent, Thou
in thine ire. But when in heart they shall re - pent, Thou
in thine ire. But when in heart they shall re - pent, Thou

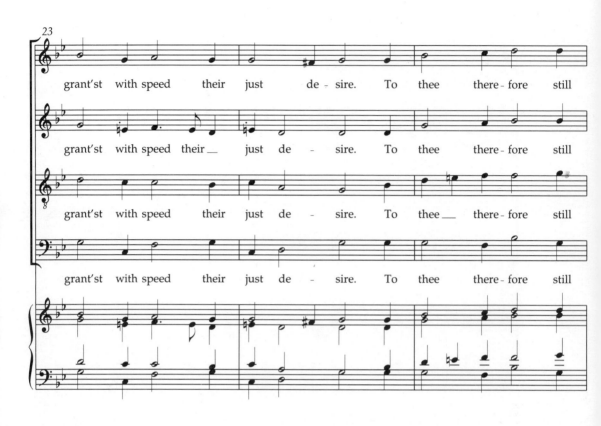

blood, O Lord, is not yet dry, But that it may help me in time.

blood, O Lord, is not yet dry, But that it may help me in time.

blood, O Lord, is not yet dry, But that it may help me in time.

blood, O Lord, is not yet dry, But that it may help me in time.

VERSE 3: The Eglantine Table Version

Haste thee,[5] O Lord, haste thee,[5] I say, To

Haste thee,[5] O Lord, haste thee,[5] I say, To

Haste thee,[5] O Lord, haste thee,[5] I say, To

Haste thee,[5] O Lord, haste thee,[5] I say, To

[5] **Day**: now

⁸ **Chirk**: E natural

Critical Commentary

O Lord, in thee is all my trust was widely known in sixteenth- and seventeenth-century Britain as a monophonic devotional song. From 1562 until the early eighteenth century it was included in editions of Sternhold and Hopkins's popular metrical psalter under the following heading:

> Through perfect repentance, the sinner hath a sure trust in God that his sins shall be washed away in Christ's blood.

The tune is unascribed, but it is possibly the work of Thomas Tallis: a four-part harmonization attributed to 'M[aster?] Talys' was in existence by or soon after 1550, a decade before the melody passed into editions of Sternhold and Hopkins.

Although at least three distinct versions of Tallis's setting were in use by the mid 1560s, they are so closely related to one another that the variants must be due to wilful changes, corruptions, and ornamentations introduced during the course of transmission, not (as is so often the case with Tallis) to the composer's change of mind. This edition makes use of all three versions, set respectively to the three verses of the text. Obvious errors in the various sources, and spelling, capitalization, and punctuation of the texts, have been adjusted without further note.

VERSE 1: The Day/Chirk Castle Version

The most severely plain and probably the earliest version was printed by John Day in his *Certaine Notes* (London, 1560/1565) and *Mornyng and Evenyng Prayer* (London, 1565), a collection originally intended for publication in or soon after 1550, but finally issued only in 1565 (see John Aplin, 'The Origins of John Day's "Certaine Notes"', *Music and Letters*, 62 [1981], 295). The version in the Chirk Castle partbooks (New York, Public Library, MS Mus. Res. *MNZ [Chirk]; copied *c*.1620–35) differs from Day's only in its insistence on E naturals in the Alto part, giving the music a strong dorian flavour. Other sources (used for verses 2 and 3) vacillate over the question of modality; one also inclines towards dorian while the other is inconsistent in its addition of E flats. The edition of the first verse follows Chirk, but performers should feel free to flat certain E naturals (marked with asterisks) and adjust verses 2 and 3 as they see fit.

In Day, the Soprano melody in verse 2 is lightly ornamented in bars 2, 4, and 16:

In verse 3 only, both Day and Chirk indicate a repeat of the music of the final couplet; this has been incorporated into the edition at bars 45–8. The concluding 'Amen' (bars 49–50) is unique to the Day/Chirk Castle Version. The following accidentals are missing in Day: Soprano, 1.4, 2.2, 4.2, 8.2, 10.2, 12.2, 16.2; Alto, 14.4. Small rhythmic variants between the three verses, accommodating different stress-patterns in the text, have not been noted.

VERSE 2: The 'Parsons's Psalter' Version

While *Certaine Notes* lingered in the press, Day published an alternative version of Tallis's setting in *The Whole Psalmes in Foure Parts* (London, 1563). This book, a selection of devotional pieces for domestic use, is closely associated with William Parsons, who composed much of the music and may have acted as editor, and it is commonly known as 'Parsons's Psalter'. The reading differs from that of Day/Chirk in three respects. First, music is provided for the first verse only (the remaining text would have been supplied by a copy of Sternhold and Hopkins), and in the present edition the texting of verse 2 is editorial throughout. Second, each of the eight end-of-line cadences (bars 18, 20, etc.) is marked with a fermata; these have been suppressed in the edition. Third, the inner parts are lightly ornamented with passing-notes. In the copy at Brasenose College, Oxford, the first note of the Tenor has been erased and changed (in ink) to B flat.

VERSE 3: The Eglantine Table Version

The third version is known only from a carved, inlaid panel in the Eglantine Table at Hardwick Hall, Derbyshire, where the music is shown in pseudo-score. Made to celebrate the triple wedding between the Talbot and Cavendish families in 1567, the table is richly decorated with images of music and musical instruments; see David Collins, 'A 16th–Century Manuscript in Wood', *Early Music*, 4 (1976), 275–9. Owing to wear and darkening of the wood, a few notes and accidentals are obscure or missing, and their transcription is conjectural. Nevertheless, most of the music is clearly legible, and it reveals an elaborate reading which may have been intended for instruments. Ranges are unusually wide for voices, the melodic lines are ornamented in a manner suggestive of instrumental embellishment, and no text is given beyond the incipit; the adaptation to verse 3 is editorial throughout. (In bar 46, minims in all four voices have been broken into two crotchets to accomodate the word 'continually'.) As in the Day/Chirk Castle Version, repeat signs are given at bar 45; the implication is that the final couplet of all three verses was repeated. In line with the 'Parsons's Psalter' Version, fermatas placed at the end of each phrase of music—inconsistently applied in the Eglantine Table—have been removed.

Performance Practice

Tallis may have conceived the work as a devotional song for domestic performance, with or without instrumental participation; both 'Parsons's Psalter' and the Eglantine Table support this interpretation. However, the presence of the piece in Day's *Certaine Notes* and the Chirk Castle partbooks implies that it was also sung in churches as a hymn or anthem, and choral performance is an acceptable alternative. In this edition the pitch has been chosen to accomodate the unusually wide ranges of the Eglantine Table Version; in practice, a slightly lower pitch (with octave transpositions of the Bass in verse 3 where necessary) may be more comfortable for modern church choirs.

O nata lux de lumine

Edited by Anthony Greening
Hymn at Lauds, Transfiguration

THOMAS TALLIS
(*c*.1505-85)

Source: William Byrd and Thomas Tallis, *Cantiones . . . sacrae.* (London, 1575), no. 8.

Translation: O Light of light, by love inclined,
Jesu, redeemer of mankind,
With loving-kindness deign to hear
From suppliant voices praise and prayer.

Thou who to raise our souls from hell
Didst deign in fleshly form to dwell,
Vouchsafe us, when our race is run,
In thy fair Body to be one.

O sacrum convivium

Edited by John Milsom
Vespers Antiphon, Corpus Christi

THOMAS TALLIS
(c.1505–85)

Translation

O sacred feast in which the body of Christ is consumed, the memory of his passion is brought to mind, the mind is filled with grace, and a pledge of the glory to come is given to us.

Source

William Byrd and Thomas Tallis, *Cantiones . . . sacrae* (London, 1575), no. 9. *O sacrum convivium* was probably composed in the 1560s, but, like several other motets included by Tallis in his 1575 collection, it was later substantially revised. The music was originally conceived as an instrumental fantasia; subsequently, during the course of its extensive musical remoulding, it was adapted to a variety of English texts—not necessarily added by Tallis himself—as well as to the present Latin words. The version published in 1575 may be regarded as Tallis's final, definitive statement on the work. For a discussion of the various stages of its evolution and a selective listing of variant readings in early sources, see John Milsom, 'A Tallis Fantasia', *The Musical Times*, 126 (1985), 658–62, and 'Tallis's First and Second Thoughts', *Journal of the Royal Musical Association*, 113 (1988), 203–22.

O salutaris hostia

Edited by John Milsom
Verse 5 of 'Verbum supernum prodiens'
(Hymn at Lauds, Corpus Christi)

THOMAS TALLIS
(*c*.1505–85)

Translation: O saving Victim! opening wide
The gate of heaven to man below,
Our foes press hard on every side;
Thine aid supply, thy strength bestow.

Sources

There is evidence to suggest that Tallis reworked the music of *O salutaris hostia* at least once; but unlike other motets of its kind that similarly underwent revision, including *O sacrum convivium* and *Salvator mundi*, he never published it in a definitive form. The many manuscript copies in which it survives are frequently in disagreement with one another, sometimes on account of errors introduced during the process of transmission which later scribes attempted to rectify by guesswork, and sometimes on account of ornamentation of the melodic lines.

The present edition attempts to reconstruct the motet as it existed in its 'revised' state before the process of contamination began. Close attention has been paid to the original form of the work, which survives uniquely—but with some obvious errors—in London, British Library, Additional MS 31390 (hereafter **A**), copied *c*.1580. The following sources, which all transmit versions of the revised score, have been consulted:

B Cambridge, King's College, Rowe MS 316 (*c*.1570): Alto only.
C London, British Library, MS additions to printed book K.3.b.15 (*c*.1570): all five parts.
D Oxford, Christ Church, Mus. 984–8 (*c*.1581): all five parts.
E Oxford, Bodleian Library, Tenbury MS 389, and a MS in the private possession of Mr David McGhie (the 'James' MS) (late 16th century): Soprano and Tenor only. Also London, British Library, Additional MS 23624, a copy of the work scored up by John Alcock in *c*.1763, using the complete original set before the loss of the other partbooks.
F London, British Library, Additional MSS 30480–4 (last quarter of 16th century): all five parts.
G London, British Library, Additional MS 22597 (late 16th century): Baritone only.
H Various partbooks and lutebooks associated with Edward Paston (late 16th and early 17th century): Chelmsford, Essex Record Office, MS D/DP.Z6/1; London, British Library, Additional MSS 29247 and 34049; London, Royal College of Music, MS 2089; Oxford, Bodleian Library, Tenbury MSS 431–4 and 1469–71.

The edition follows sources **B–H** when they are unanimous in their readings. When they diverge over what are evidently transmission errors, source **A** has usually been followed. All inconsistencies of underlay (and small rhythmic variants needed to accomodate them) have been eliminated without further comment. Ornamentations of the melodic lines are similarly suppressed. The following commentary is selective, reporting only some of the most significant variants.

Critical Commentary

S, 13.2, **C–F**: A for E / S, 25.5 and 29.5, **A**: in each case, G added over erased A / Tenor, 34.3–35.1: miscopied as EF for ED early in the course of transmission. Sources **B–H** variously correct the passage by rewriting either the Alto or the Tenor during bars 34–7. The edition follows **A** / A, 41.2, **E** and **H**: cC sharp, cD, cA for m.A / S, 42.4, **F** and **H**: G for D / bars 48–9: in **A**, the cadence extends over only four crotchet beats (equivalent to omitting the second half of bar 48)

Purge me, O Lord

Edited by John Milsom
Words: anon., mid-16th-century

THOMAS TALLIS
(c.1505–85)

Sources

A London, British Library, Add. MSS 30480–3 (complete set of four partbooks, c.1565).

B London, British Library, Add. MS 30513 (the 'Mulliner Book', copied by Thomas Mulliner c.1550–75; keyboard reduction of all four voice-parts).

Critical Commentary

Purge me, O Lord is a devotional partsong rather than an anthem, and there is no evidence that it was sung in churches during Tallis's lifetime. The source of the words is unknown. The present edition largely follows source **A**; for a diplomatic transcription of the version in source **B**, see *The Mulliner Book*, ed. Denis Stevens, *Musica Britannica* 1 (London, 2/1954), no.25. In source **B** the piece is inexplicably titled 'Fond youth is a bubble', and it was on the basis of this that Edward Thomas Warren, in a collection of c.1800, provided alternative words to the music, with the note that 'the words are adapted anew' (Oxford, Bodleian Library, Tenbury MS 958). Warren's adaptation has been included in *Thomas Tallis, English Sacred Music: I. Anthems*, ed. Leonard Ellinwood, rev. Paul Doe, *Early English Church Music* 12 (London, 2/1973), no.16.

A, 5.1–2, **A**: F sharp implied / B, 5.3, **B**: F sharp implied / A, 7.2: D sharp in **B** only / Bar 9: **B** has the following accidentals:

 S and A, 10.3–11.4, **B**:

A, 19.2, both sources: F sharp implied / B, 21.2: F sharp implied in **B** only / B, 23.4: F natural specified in **A**, F sharp implied in **B** / T and B, 24.1–2, **B**: cc

Salvator mundi

Edited by John Milsom
Matins antiphon, Exaltation of the Cross

THOMAS TALLIS
(*c*.1505–85)

Source: William Byrd and Thomas Tallis, *Cantiones . . . sacrae* (London, 1575), no. 1.
Translation: Saviour of the world, save us, who by your cross and your blood has redeemed us; help us, we beseech you, our God.

Te lucis ante terminum

Edited by Simon R. Hill
Compline hymn

1. FESTAL TONE

THOMAS TALLIS
(*c*.1505–85)

3. Prae - sta, Pa - ter om - ni - po - tens, Per Je - sum Chri - stum __ Do - mi - num;

Qui te-cum in __ per-pe-tu-um __ Reg-nat cum Sanc-to Spi-ri - tu. A - men. __

2. FERIAL TONE

Source: William Byrd and Thomas Tallis, *Cantiones . . . sacrae* (London, 1575), no. 20.

Text: Office hymn at Compline, from Trinity to Lent, except on double feasts and their octaves and Christmas Eve to the octave of Epiphany.

For commemorations of the BVM verse 3 is: Gloria tibi, Domine,
Qui natus es de Virgine,
Cum Patre et Sancto Spiritu,
In sempiterna saecula.

Verily, verily, I say unto you

Edited by
Anthony Greening

John 6:53–6

THOMAS TALLIS
(*c*.1505–85)

Sources

A London, British Library, Additional MS 15166 (*c*.1570): S only.

B Cambridge, Peterhouse, MSS 34, 38, 39 (*c*.1635): S, A, and B only.

C Ely, Cathedral Library, MS 1 (*c*.1635): Organ.

D Ely, Cathedral Library, MS 28 (mid-17th-century): T only.

Critical Commentary

Accidentals in the soprano part, which are largely absent from **A** (the earliest source), have been supplied from **B** and **C** without further note. Small rhythmic variants in **C**, which is a partial reduction of the voice-parts for organ, have also not been recorded. For a more detailed critical commentary see *Thomas Tallis, English Sacred Music: 1, Anthems*, ed. Leonard Ellinwood, rev. Paul Doe, *Early English Church Music*, 12 (London, 1973), no. 10.

5

-cept ye eat the flesh of the Son of man, and drink his_ blood, ye have

-cept ye eat the flesh of the Son of man, and drink his blood, ye have

-cept ye eat the flesh of the Son_ of man, and_ drink his_ blood, ye have

-cept ye eat the flesh of the Son of man, and drink his blood, ye

10

no life in_____ you. Who - - so eat - eth my flesh,_

no life in_____ you. Who - - so eat - eth my flesh,

no life in_____ you. Who - - so eat - eth my flesh,_

have no life in you. Who - - so eat - eth my flesh,_

¹ all sources: m c-rest for m.

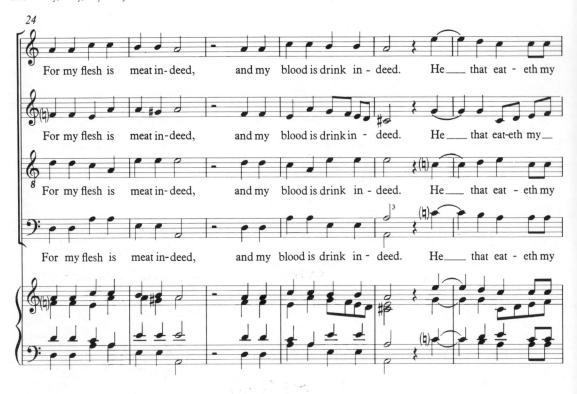

³ B: *sic;* the upper A is presumably optional